KEYWORD RESEARCH

How To Find And Profit From
Low Competition Long Tail
Keywords

+

33 Profitable Niches Analysed

NATHAN GEORGE

DEDICATION

To the memory of my parents, John and Esther.

CONTENTS

1 INTRODUCTION

Keyword research is the practice of finding and analysing actual search terms people enter into search engines when carrying out searches online. With this information you get to see real customer activity to enable you figure out what potential customers are looking for online and also importantly, what they're not looking for.

Keyword research helps you to find the right niche to enter based on real stats on current customer behaviour, rather than guess work or speculation.

Niche research and selection is one of the most important aspects of your online business. You could get everything else right, like product creation and marketing, but if you've selected a niche that is just not in demand or the niche is too saturated to get noticed, then the whole thing fails.

What people tend to do is create a product first and then try to find customers to sell it to online. The problem is people are not just going to stumble on your site.

There are so many sites and products on the internet with no traffic and sales. Most people fail online because they simply do not carry out niche research before creating a product or service.

You may think you know what you're doing because you believe the product you're creating is generally in demand, so there are bound to be customers right? Not necessarily!

I made this same mistake on my first product. I spent about 6 months creating a PDF eBook and a website on dating and relationships and thought I couldn't fail as there will always be an audience for this niche. Well it didn't work because I failed to identify who exactly my customers were; what kind of phrases they were searching for online; the number of potential customers; if I could actually compete in that niche against the other established products/sites etc.

I wasted 6 months on that venture and hardly made any sales. No amount of marketing or tweaking of my sales copy made any difference.

After learning this lesson I now make research (and sometimes even testing) my number one priority before I start any project. I now run several profitable websites making me passive income (from affiliate product sales and AdSense) that I built purely on keyword research.

I learnt from my costly mistake but you can avoid all that with the information I'll share with you in this book.

First identify your market EXACTLY, not vaguely in your head, not from assumptions about what you think people want, but from actual statistical figures obtained from research and analysis of the competition to see if you can actually compete and be noticed in the niche.

Niche selection is also a personal thing as we all have different interests and skills. It is important to select a niche you can stick with over the long run - good and bad times. Money alone is not sufficient as a motivator. You need to have enough interest in the topic to be able to spend a significant amount of time on it creating content and providing value to customers.

If you don't get your niche right nothing you do after matters. You could have an excellent product and perform all kinds of marketing tricks but it will all come to nothing.

You could find many sources online with lists of supposedly "profitable niches" but as the saying goes:

"Give a man a fish and you feed him for a day; teach a man to fish and you feed him for a lifetime."

As things change so quickly on the internet it is best to learn for yourself how to fish for profitable niches and this is what you'll get from this book.

2 ADOPT THE MINDSET OF A MARKETER

To be successful in this business you have to put on the hat of a marketer. The mistake I made when I first started was that I saw myself as an "artist" or "creator". I created my products and then tried to convince people to buy them.

So I was putting myself first and creating what I wanted to create and hoping the market will acquiesce to me. The problem was that the market did not exactly agree with me and I wasn't able to convince many people to buy my "art".

So to approach this from a purely marketing perspective, the first thing to do is to forget about what you want and focus on what the market wants.

Think of a traditional marketer like a grocery shop owner for example. From experience the shop owner would know the products that sell and those that don't sell so he would only stock those that people would actually buy. He would not stock products just because he is passionate about them.

As an Internet Marketer you're like the digital

equivalent of the traditional trader. You first find out what customers want, then you go and acquire it (or create your version of it), and give it to them. You focus on the customer and their needs. Your own needs do not matter.

To succeed in business in general you have to HELP people. You have to help a lot of people. So the question becomes, how do you find people to help? The answer is: Keyword Research.

Many people searching online are looking for help in whatever area they're searching on. If you find enough people searching online on a particular subject area then you can offer them help in the form of a product or service.

Note that as a marketer you do not necessarily have to create the solution yourself. You could source it from an expert on the subject matter, and your job is to package it and effectively market it to customers.

You're trading online so the best way to find people you can help in your business is to capture and analyse what people are searching for online using the search engines.

You need to provide customers with what they need, and not what you think they need. You may be surprised to discover that what you think the market needs does not match up with the realities in the market and what's really in demand. Hence you actually need to carry out market research and identify specific needs in the market before creating products to match them.

If what you're passionate about marries up with a specific need in the market then that is great, however trying to be "innovative" is not going to get you far as a beginner. I know this from personal experience and what I have seen from many others.

Don't try to create a cash stream, instead find a cash

stream that's already flowing and position yourself where some of that cash is flowing towards you.

Finally, even though you're putting the customer's needs first, it is important to choose an area that you have an interest in. It does not need to be your passion but you need to be interested enough to be spending a significant amount of time creating value on it.

It is difficult to get motivated by what you have absolutely no interest in, especially if you may need to spend a couple of months or even years on the niche, like a website for example. Money alone does not provide the required motivation, particularly when times are tough and you're not seeing any results yet.

3 THE NICHE TEST

I first heard of the "Niche Test" from one of my mentors, Eben Pagan. I modified it slightly for my own purposes and have used it successfully ever since.

There are 4 questions you test a niche against before you proceed with it.

Throughout the process of selecting and analysing a niche idea you need to be asking these questions. If you get a YES for all 4 questions then you've got a product or niche that you ought to look at. If you don't get a yes to all 4 questions then you need to keep working at the idea until you get yes to all of them.

1. Is Your Customer Experiencing Pain And Urgency Or Irrational Passion?

Do they have a strong emotional need?

Here are some examples of what I mean by a strong emotional need:

David, 30, Admin Officer

David is suffering from a bad credit score. Over the last few years he has used his credit cards up to the limit and is now struggling to make repayments. His debt situation is a constant stress in his life and his marriage is already suffering because of it. He has reached a point where he is now **desperate** *to get himself out of this predicament and back into financial stability.*

Amy, 18, Student

Amy is suffering from cystic acne. She has tried nearly every product out there but only gets brief relief without finding a cure. She is at a point now where she is so **embarrassed** *with her condition that she avoids socials situations and even makes excuses to skip classes when she has a really bad breakout. She is* **desperate** *for a solution.*

Jeff, 50, Painter

Jeff has worked as a builder for many years and loves his job. Recently he sustained and injury when he fell off a ladder and injured his back. He is now in pain for most of the day and this is affecting his ability to work. Jeff is worried about not being able to work as he is the sole breadwinner in the family. Being unable to work will be devastating to his family and he is **desperate** *for any advice and information regarding dealing with his back pain.*

As you can see from the highlighted words, these people all have one thing in common. They all have a strong emotional need to solve their problems. This is what will drive them to spend money to solve their problems.

2. Is Your Customer Actively Searching The Internet For A Solution?

You don't want to be in the position of trying to talk them into wanting what you are selling. Look for customers who are looking for you. And since we will be marketing our products on the internet it is important to check that people are actively searching the internet for solutions. We cover this later with the Google Keyword Planner and other tools.

3. Does Your Customer Have Few Or No Perceived Options?

You want your niche narrow and focused enough that there are not many options out there for customers in this niche. A niche that is too saturated is very difficult to get noticed in, no matter how good your product is.

When they find your solution they should feel they haven't seen something quite like it somewhere else. Basically you need to have a unique angle to what you're providing, a unique selling proposition (USP).

4. Is Your Customer Willing To Pay For A Solution To The Problem?

If we have determined that people are actively looking for a solution the next question is, are people willing to pay for the solution?

For some issues people search the internet for free information and are not necessarily willing to pay for something. The best way to find out if money is being made in the niche is to check if other marketers are making money in it. You might think this is the opposite of what we want. After all shouldn't we be happy with a niche with little or no competition? The reality though is that if you can't see other marketers already present and successfully making money in that niche it is very likely there is little money to be made in it. There are several ways to check this and we'll be covering it in detail later in the book.

4 NARROW DOWN YOUR NICHE

As a beginner when you're thinking of creating a product or service the instinctive thing to do is to make it cover as wide an area as possible. After all it seems to make more sense to make your product or service attractive to as many people as possible.

The reality is that this is actually the wrong thing to be doing. What you really need to be doing is the opposite i.e. narrowing down the niche.

Research shows that when we have a problem that we're urgently seeking a solution for we tend to buy things that sound like they were made to fix our specific problem and not a "cure all" solution. This could be because the specific solution appears to be more specifically tailored to the problem than a "fix all" solution that might have been watered down so it fits everything.

So if you have a "fix all" product or service you'll actually attract fewer customers and not more.

Also, when a niche is too large and competitive it is very difficult to get noticed and make any money as a beginner. Even if the niche is popular with a huge demand in the market, if you have too much competition it is hard to get noticed above all the noise in the market.

It doesn't matter how good your product is, if you can't rank in the search engines for any of the terms related to your product or service you'll have a hard time making money.

The Three Big Niches

If you're creating an information product you want to stay within the 3 big niches where most of the money online is made. These 3 big areas generate billions of dollars a year in sales.

1. Lifestyle

2. Business and Money

3. Health and Fitness

These 3 areas are where people usually have a desperate, urgent or passionate need to solve a problem. Now these are pretty broad niches and you don't want to create a product or service directly for any of these. Rather, you want to start from inside these 3 big niches then narrow down to a sub-niche.

For example some sub-niches under these mega niches are:

Lifestyle
- Personal Development
- Dating Advice
- Home Improvement & DIY
- Art, Antiques & Hobbies
- Divorce
- Dog Training

Business and Money
- Starting A Business
- Forex Trading
- Investing
- Debt
- Making Money
- Internet Marketing

Health and Fitness
- Fitness Instructor
- Stress
- Raw Foods
- Fat Loss
- Vegan Diet Recipes
- Organic Food

We'll cover more of these sub-niches later in the book.

Always Go At Least Three Steps Down

Category => Niche => Sub-Niche

Let's take an example from the Health & Fitness niche:

Health & Fitness => Weight Loss => Losing Weight after Pregnancy

Health & Fitness is a big niche with a lot of money being made yearly. However if you try to enter that niche you'll simply be unable to compete with the major players with a lot of money and prestige. You'll simply not be able to rank in the search engines for those general terms.

When you go a niche down to Weight Loss it is pretty much the same thing. You'll have to compete with popular names like Dr Oz, Weight Watchers, celebrities, and other big companies with loads of money for marketing so it'll be difficult to get noticed.

Now if you go down a niche to a sub-category of weight loss, for example, Losing Weight after Pregnancy, you get a smaller niche specific to women looking to lose weight after pregnancy.

The good thing is that the big players with huge budgets will consider a niche like this too small for them. They want larger audiences so will not restrict themselves to a small area of specialisation. And this is good for you because the niche still gets a decent amount of searches per month and you're more likely to be able to compete against the other players in the niche.

Let's take another example:

Cooking => Baking => Gluten Free Baking

Cooking is a huge market but very competitive. Go one step deeper to Baking but it'll still be too competitive with a lot of baking resources out there.

Now if you go one niche deeper to a specific problem or trend within baking, you come up with Gluten Free Baking. It'll be so much easier to become an authority on gluten free baking than it would be on general cooking or general baking. You'll have a motivated audience seeking specific products, advice and recommendations. If you can fill that need then it would be a great opportunity.

Now let's look at a final example.

Sports => Basketball => High School Basketball

With a website on Sports in general you'll have to compete with the major sports networks like ESPN, CBS Sports, SKY Sports etc. As a small player in the field it'll be impossible to build a brand as a sports network and compete with these guys.

You could specifically niche down to say Basketball but that too would be way too saturated as there are so many basketball oriented sites out there that it'll be hard to get noticed above all the noise.

Now you could niche down to a sub-niche within basketball, High School Basketball. There are still tons of people interested in high school basketball and you could become a real authority there. The opportunity there as an affiliate will be to promote things like high school coaching programs, programs that teach high school coaches training techniques, products on fitness and training related to basketball, and a whole array of products to do with fitness and basketball.

So as you can see from the examples above, if you want to make money in this business it is very important to niche down. You don't want a field that's too saturated and competitive.

Even if you have money to spend on advertising you'll not be able to outspend the major players in the niche so it'll be very difficult to establish a position of authority.

If you niche down then you get some very interesting sub-niches with a decent audience size. The good news is that big businesses are not so interested in these small niches but they are perfect for us.

5 USEFUL WEBSITES TO BRAINSTORM FOR IDEAS

1. About.com

Website: http://www.about.com

Scroll down to the bottom of the page to the area titled

"EVERYTHING ON ABOUT.COM"

Fig. 1

This list provides a treasure trove of topics to choose

from. This is like an index of topics.

Note down topics that resonate with you. You don't have to be passionate about the topic and it doesn't need to be the love of your life. But to create a product or service around an idea and do all the necessary work involved, you want something you at least have some interest in. The importance of this can never be overstated.

I am not saying each topic you find here will be profitable but you can get ideas from here and then carry out further research on them to see if they're profitable. I will show you how to do that in this book.

2. Alltop.com

Website: http://alltop.com

Go through the alphabets from A - Z and you'll be able to see some interesting ideas from the Results section.

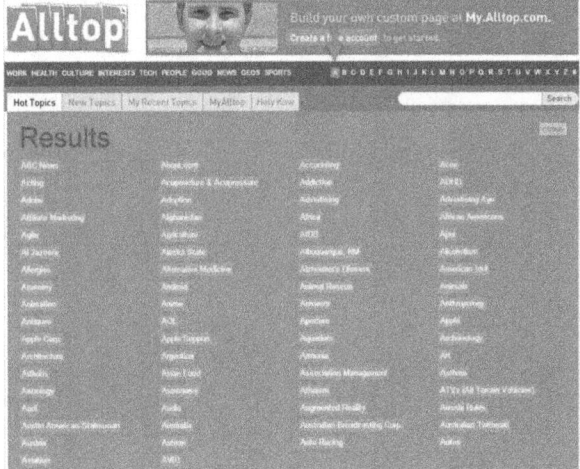

Fig. 2

3. Dummies.com

Website: http://www.dummies.com

Dummies.com is another great site to brainstorm niche ideas. They do a lot of research to ensure a topic is profitable before publishing a book on it. So they've essentially done all the research for you because if you see a Dummies book on a given topic then it's very likely to be a profitable niche.

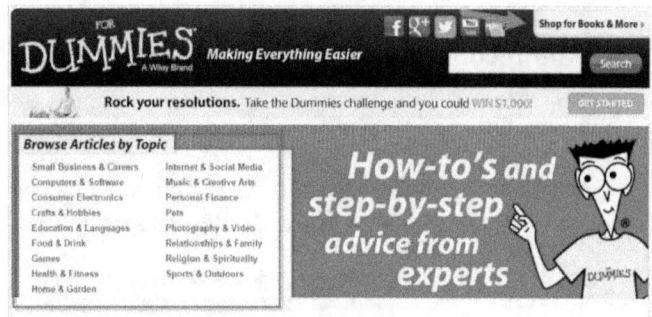

Fig. 3

Click on Shop for Books & More.

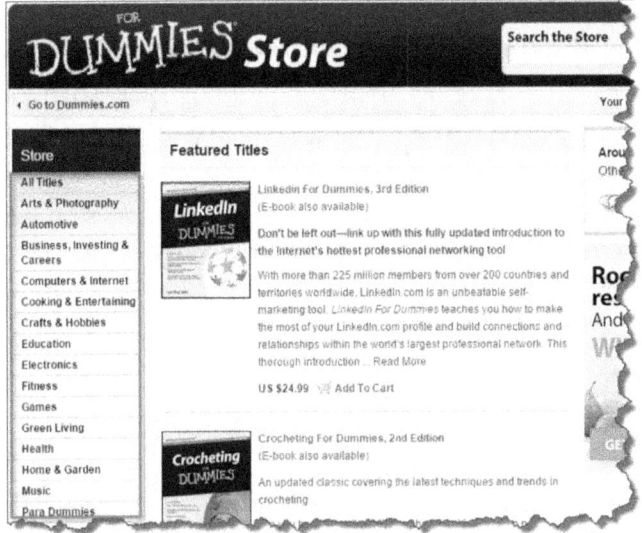

Fig. 4

Click on the categories to explore the books in each. Remember each one would be on a topic that has been researched and seen to be profitable by Dummies.com.

4. Amazon.com

Website: http://www.amazon.com

Amazon is another place you can use for researching niche ideas. Make sure you go to Amazon.com and not a local version like Amazon.co.uk or Amazon.ca, if you live outside the USA. This is because the main audience on Amazon is on Amazon.com.

If people are creating magazines on a topic it means that the area is profitable because it costs a lot of time, effort and money to produce magazines, so they make sure they carry out thorough research before making that kind of investment in it.

Go to Shop by Department > Books and Audible > Magazines

To brainstorm for ideas, browse the categories on the left hand side. You'll find hundreds of topics there to get ideas from.

Fig. 5

Click on Best Sellers to view the most popular topics in each category.

Fig. 6

These four sites are more than enough for brainstorming niche ideas. Of course there are many other resources out there you could use to find niche ideas but you don't want to overdo it as it could turn to analysis paralysis.

Once you've done the brainstorming and selecting one or more niche areas what you want to do next is to analyse in more detail the audience size, profitability and also to find the best keywords to use with the niche. We can do this using various tools.

6 THE FREE TOOLS YOU NEED

In this chapter I'll outline the tools you need for keyword research and indicate where registration is required to gain access to a tool. This is so that by the time we come to use them in this book you have already registered and can follow the examples.

1. Google Keyword Planner

Link: https://adwords.google.com/KeywordPlanner

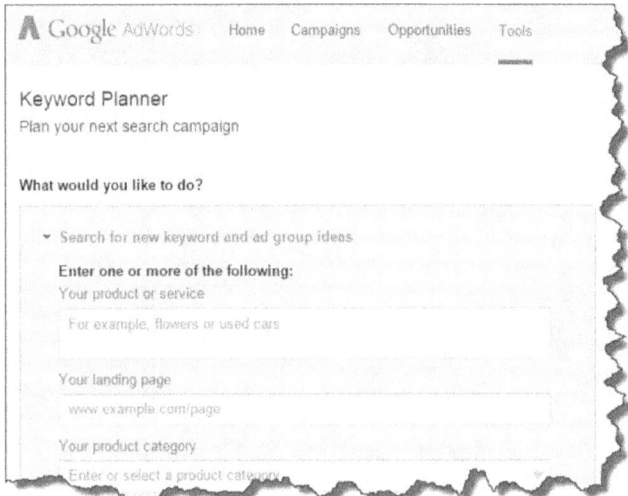

Fig. 7

The Google Keyword Planner is actually for advertisers who want to use Google AdWords to research and bid for paid ads. These ads then show up in the sponsored sections of Google when someone searches for those keywords.

You'll need to sign up for an AdWords account if you don't have one already. Even though you're not bidding for paid ads you can still use the tool to research your keywords and get ideas for long tail keywords. Registration is free.

2. MOZ.com

Link for signup: https://moz.com/products/api/keys

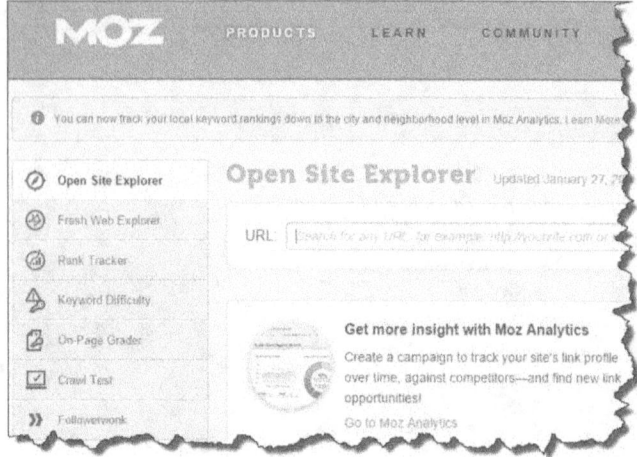

Fig. 8

MOZ.com is a website that provides some free tools that you can use to analyse competitor websites and get some stats to figure out their "strength" in terms of search engine ranking and competitiveness.

Moz.com allows you to view website stats like: Domain Authority, Page Authority, Back Links, and Inbound Links.

Although they offer some paid services, the particular tool you'll need for your research is free. Registration is free. After you register you get issued API Credentials (an Access ID and a Secret Key).

Link to their Open Site Explorer tool which is the one we're interested in:

https://moz.com/researchtools/ose/

3. SEMrush

Link: http://www.semrush.com/

Fig. 9

When you enter a keyword in SEMrush it provides the information you already get with Google Keyword Planner, including a list of the top 10 sites ranking for that keyword.

You can also view stats on individual websites over the last 12 months like organic keywords, Ads keywords, search engine traffic and Ads traffic. You can view a list of keywords bringing the most traffic to the website and get keyword ideas you can use on your own site to target search engine traffic.

Other Free Keyword Suggestion Tools - Optional

4. Keyword Tool

Link: http://keywordtool.io/

Fig. 10

Keyword Tool is a free online keyword research tool that uses the Google Autocomplete function to generate hundreds of long-tail keywords relevant to your seed phrase.

Google Autocomplete is a feature in Google Search which suggests terms as you type in the search bar. The search terms that are suggested by Google Autocomplete are based on many factors including how often users searched for a particular term in the past. See example in image below.

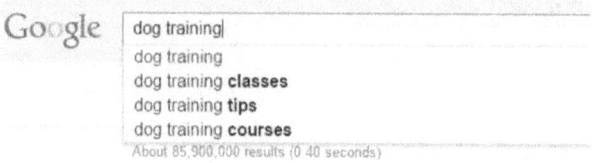

Fig. 11

The Autocomplete function in Google provides a real

time drop down list of the 10 most searched phrases related to the word or phrase you're typing in. The Keyword Tool gives you this same information for hundreds of keywords that you can copy to a file and analyse in your own time to find long tail keywords suitable for your needs.

We don't need the Keyword Tool for the keyword research we'll be covering in this book. However it comes in handy if you want more control over finding suggestions from the autocomplete list you see in google.

5. Übersuggest

Link: http://www.ubersuggest.org/

With this free keyword tool you can instantly get thousands of keyword ideas from real user searches. Similar to Keyword Tool above, the long tail keywords you get from Ubersugest are extracted from the Autocomplete data in Google. You can use this to get keywords to inspire your next article or blog post.

Again, like Keyword Tool, it is not necessary to use this tool for keyword research, especially if you're using Google Keyword Planner. However it is a good alternative for mining for keywords from the autocomplete list in google.

7 USING GOOGLE SEARCH OPERATORS

If you want a more detailed search, with options to enter additional filters, you can use the Google Advanced Search engine which provides more search fields and options to customise your search.

http://www.google.com/advanced_search

You can also use the following Google Search Operators for more specific searches.

https://support.google.com/websearch/answer/2466433?hl=en

Search Operator	Advanced Search Features
filetype:	File Format
allintitle:	Occurrences in the title of the page
allintext:	Occurrences in the text of the page
allinurl:	Occurrences in the URL of the page
allinanchor:	Occurrences in the links to the page
site:	Domain
related:	Similar
link:	Links

For example if you want to return only URLs that include your keyword. Enter it like this:

allinurl: [Your search keyword]

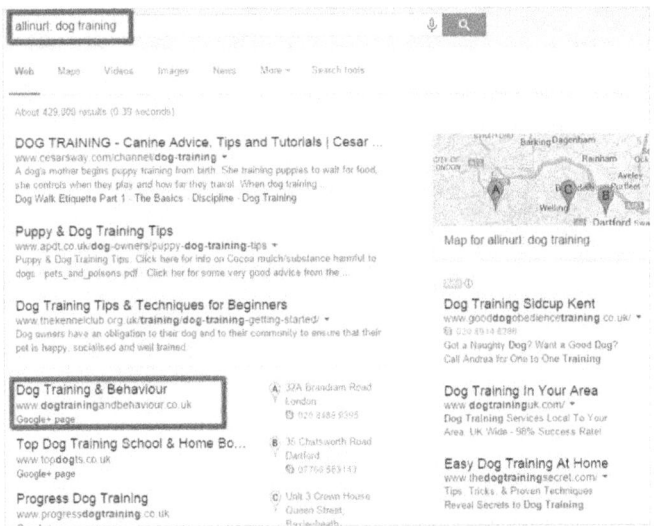

Fig. 12

For example you can check how a competitor site is

using a particular keyword so that you can get ideas for your own articles.

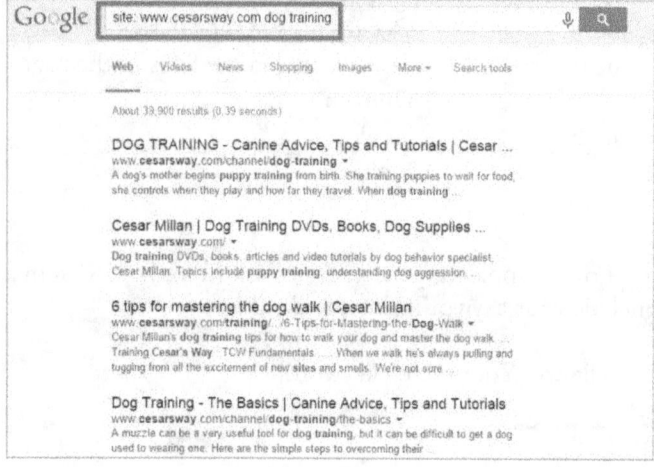

Fig. 13

8 FINDING NICHES FOR AFFILIATE MARKETING

In Chapter 3 we covered the "Niche Test" which is a test for the viability of a niche in terms of creating and selling digital information products. However if my primary reason for finding a niche is to create a website specifically for promoting affiliate products, then I have a more detailed checklist I go through to select a niche or keyword.

I ensure the keyword I choose meets the following criteria:

- I ensure the keyword gets at least 2000 local searches per month on google. By "local" I mean the USA. This is because if you're creating affiliate websites your main market will be in the USA. If you don't live in the USA and your potential customers are local (e.g. UK) then ensure your keyword is getting enough local searches. The very minimum I would recommend is 1000 local searches per month.

- The maximum search volume should be no more than 100,000 as you don't want a keyword that is too competitive. If you're a beginner I would recommend keywords no more than 15,000 searches max per month.

- The competition on google should be relatively low so that it is not too difficult to get into the top 10 search results for your keyword i.e. the first page. There are additional tools to check this and I'll cover this when we get to competitor analysis.

- There is earning potential in the niche. That is people are actually making money in the niche. We will be covering the indicators you need to look for to determine this.

- Are there physical products as well as information products for the niche? Ideally you want a niche where you can sell both physical and information products as an affiliate.

- The 50 posts test: Can I imagine myself writing 50 articles on this topic? Is there enough depth to the topic that creating content for the site will not be an issue? Other than the main keyword, are there enough related keywords with decent search volumes I can target with articles?

- Can I actually help people and provide real value for them?

9 GOOGLE KEYWORD PLANNER

Website: https://adwords.google.com/KeywordPlanner

In this chapter we will be looking at the Google Keyword Planner, which is a free keyword research tool provided by Google. As an internet marketer you'll always need to use the Google Keyword Planner even if you use paid keyword research tools.

The data we're looking at comes from google so what better tool to use than the one actually provided by google?

To start using Google Keyword Planner you first need to register with Adwords. During registration you will be asked to enter billing details but don't worry, you will not be charged anything as you will not be bidding for ads.

The Basics

For our example we'll use two seed keywords: "Raw food diet" and "Acne cure".

Ensure you set the location under "Targeting" to where most of your traffic will be coming from. In this case I have set it to the United States.

I have also filtered the Avg. Monthly searches to a minimum of 2000.

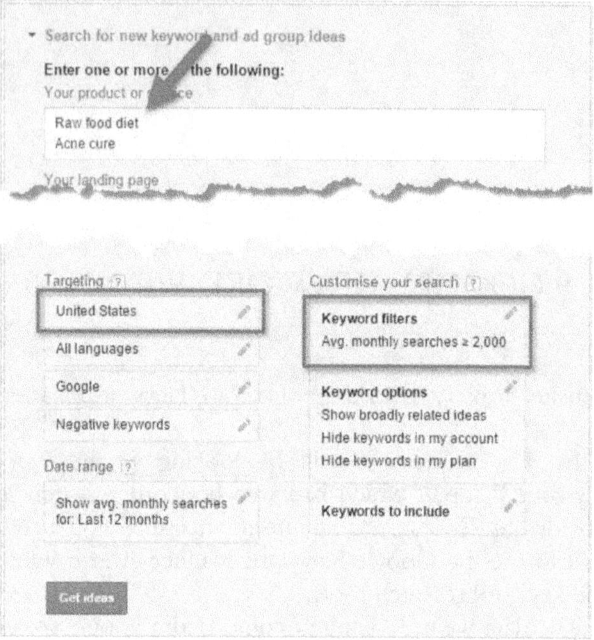

Fig. 14

When you click on Get ideas, the Keyword Planner will return a result for the seed keywords and related long tail keywords. You can see from the results below that "raw food diet" has 27,100 searches but the result for "Acne cure" is not displayed because it is less than 2000.

Ad group ideas	Keyword ideas		
Search Terms		Avg. monthly searches	Competition
raw food diet		27,100	Medium

Fig. 15

Now you might be thinking 27,100 searches for "raw food diet" is quite high hence a good niche to enter but take into account the competition in that niche.

The raw food diet niche is very competitive at the moment and it would be difficult for us to get noticed in the sea of products, websites and books out there all competing in that niche.

We need to narrow down our niche and this is where alternative keyword suggestions by the Keyword Planner come in handy.

Keyword (by relevance)	Avg. monthly searches	Competition	Suggeste
raw food diet for dogs	3,600	High	
raw food recipes	12,100	Low	
food lovers diet	9,900	High	
raw dog food	3,600	High	
raw food	4,400	Medium	
acne treatment	33,100	High	
best acne treatment	18,100	High	
acne scars	27,100	Medium	
acne scar treatment	9,900	High	
home remedies for acne	18,100	Low	
natural acne treatment	5,400	High	

Fig. 16

We can see in the image above several keywords related to the seed keywords and their monthly searches suggested by the Keyword Planner. Even though the seed keyword "Acne cure" was less than 2000 searches, hence was omitted from the main results, the Keyword Planner gives us related suggestions with more searches.

For example:
- best acne treatment - 33,100
- acne scar treatment - 9,900
- home remedies for acne - 18,100

These are very high search volumes. These kinds of phrases are referred to as "long tail keywords" as they contain more words in the search phrase. The long tails look promising so we may want to choose and further analyse one of those related keywords.

For keywords related to our "raw food diet" seed keyword, we see an interesting suggestion with a decent number of searches, "raw food diet for dogs". Now depending on what topics you're interested in, you could make a slight change here and focus on raw foods for dogs instead of raw foods for people.

Looking at the Competition column we can see that competition for advertising is "High" so this looks like a niche people are spending advertising money on.

Do not confuse "Competition" here with Search Engine Optimization (SEO) competition. This is advertiser competition. High means more advertisers are competing for this keyword.

So high competition here is actually better for us because it shows that, (1) people are spending money advertising in the niche so there is likely money being made, and (2) there is potentially a better chance of making money from AdSense ads displayed on our website.

Narrowing Your Niche

OK let's say we're looking to narrow down our niche and we decide to switch focus to "raw food diet for dogs". When we carry out a search we get the following:

Ad group ideas	**Keyword ideas**		
Search Terms		Avg. monthly searches ?	Competition ?
raw food diet for dogs		3,600	High

Keyword (by relevance)		Avg. monthly searches ?	Competition ?
raw diet for dogs		3,600	High
raw food diet		27,100	Medium
raw dog food		3,600	High
raw food		4,400	Medium
raw food recipes		12,100	Low
raw diet		5,400	Low
best dog food		27,100	High
grain free dog food		12,100	High
raw dog		2,900	Low
best dry dog food		5,400	High

Fig. 17

You can see that "raw food diet for dogs" produced a monthly search of 3,600 and also has loads of related long tail keywords with a lot of searches. This clearly is looking like a profitable niche with a lot of related long tail keywords to target with our posts or articles.

It is important to check that your niche has related keywords with a decent number of searches. This is because when you start creating articles for your website you'll be targeting some of these related keywords for your articles to help boost your search rankings.

Even though the main keyword has a decent number of searches on its own, the combined traffic from articles on your site targeting the related keywords will add up over time.

So the aim is not just to select your main keyword phrase but to keep coming back to the Keyword Planner to find related keywords with a decent amount of searches for your articles and posts on your website.

10 ARE PEOPLE MAKING MONEY IN THE NICHE?

Some of our activities during brainstorming for a seed idea already involved filtering for niches that are more likely to be profitable. I've mentioned mining for niche ideas at Dummies.com and magazines at Amazon.com. If you have not looked at these places yet then you can check them to see if there are books and magazines for your niche. Due to the production overheads involved we know these guys only get involved in topics they found to be profitable from their market research.

In addition to that you should do the following:

1. Check For Sponsored Ads In Google

Go to Google and type your idea and see if there are paid ads for the niche. If there are paid ads it is another indicator that there must be money being made in the niche as people are willing to pay for ads for it.

For example if you were researching the keyword "raw food diet for dogs", a search on Google would return results below.

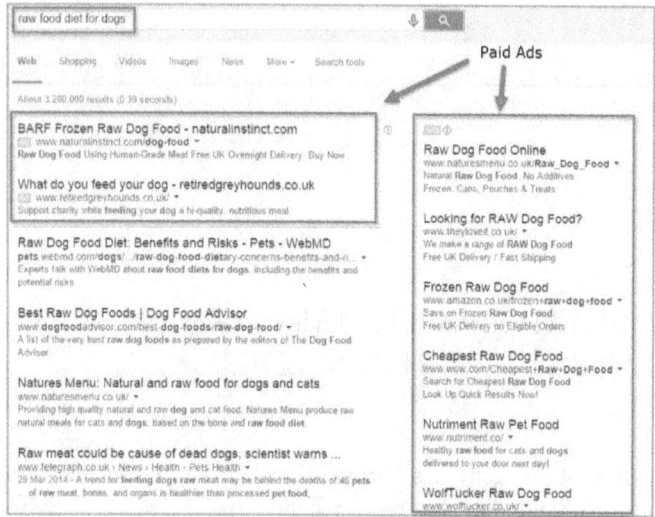

Fig. 18

The "raw food diet for dogs" niche is known to be profitable and you can see that there are quite a few ads on it when you search for that keyword. Take each of the suggested keywords from Keyword Planner you're interested in and check whether there are ads for them.

I usually make sure there are at least 3-5 ads before I proceed with a particular keyword.

If you're looking to sell affiliate products then you should also carry out the following two tests.

2. Check the Niche with a Money Related Keyword

Enter the keyword in quotes and type in a money related keyword like "price" or "affiliate". This is to see if there are any products being sold or affiliate offers in the niche.

You can see from the search below on "raw food diet" that there are no products being sold that immediately jump out.

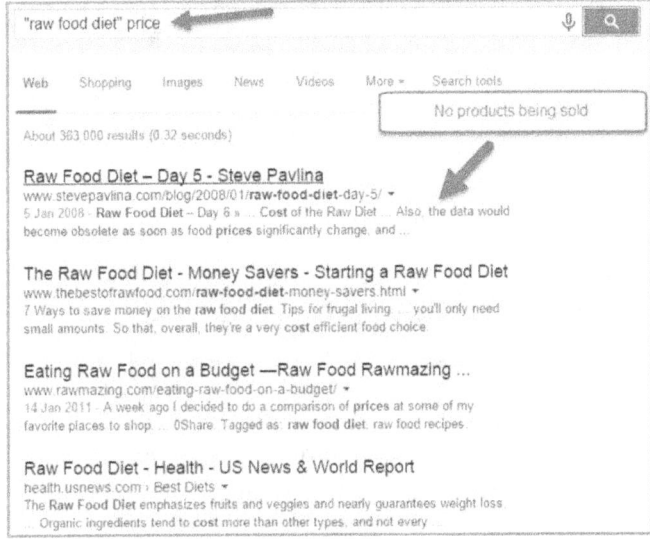

Fig. 19

3. Check ClickBank.com for Products

Link: http://www.clickbank.com/

If there are no products then it is most likely not a profitable niche. If there are products then check whether affiliates are actually making money promoting them.

You can check this by looking at the Grav (gravity) score. The higher the gravity score the more money affiliates are making from promoting the product. So if you see a lot of products in a particular niche with high gravity scores then this is a good indicator that money is being made in the niche.

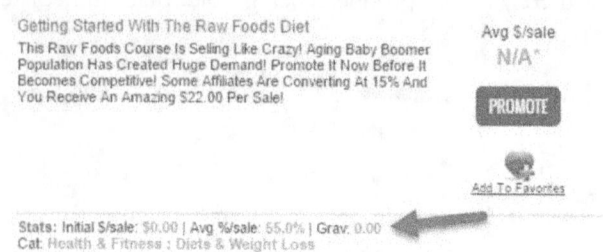

Getting Started With The Raw Foods Diet
This Raw Foods Course Is Selling Like Crazy! Aging Baby Boomer Population Has Created Huge Demand! Promote It Now Before It Becomes Competitive! Some Affiliates Are Converting At 15% And You Receive An Amazing $22.00 Per Sale!

Avg $/sale
N/A*

PROMOTE

Add To Favorites

Stats: Initial $/sale: $0.00 | Avg %/sale: 55.0% | Grav: 0.00
Cat: Health & Fitness : Diets & Weight Loss

Fig. 20

Your niche does not necessarily need to "pass" all these tests for you to decide there is money to be made in it. What methods you use to check for profitability depend on how you intend to monetize your website. If you intend to make money from AdSense then check that there are sponsored ads for the niche; if you intend to promote affiliate information products then check that there are affiliate information products being sold; if you intend to promote physical products then check that physical products are actually being sold etc.

11 GOOGLE TRENDS

An additional check you might want to carry out is how the keyword has been trending for the past few years in Google Trends.

Link: http://www.google.com/trends/

If the trend is decreasing fast then it might not be a good keyword to build a long-term product or website around. This is optional and I don't always do it unless I have some concerns regarding the longevity of the niche.

See the example below of the google trend for "raw foods recipes". You can see that the trend was at its highest around 2007 but has steadily been declining ever since. So this may not be an area you would want to go into if you're looking for something with longevity.

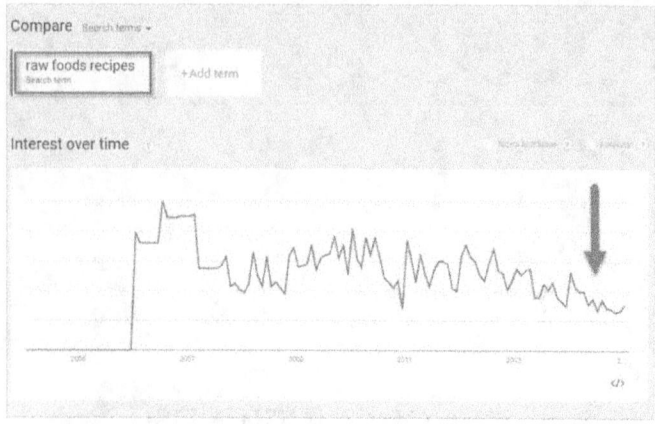

Fig. 21

On the other hand if we look at the trend (below) for "raw food diet for dogs" we get the following:

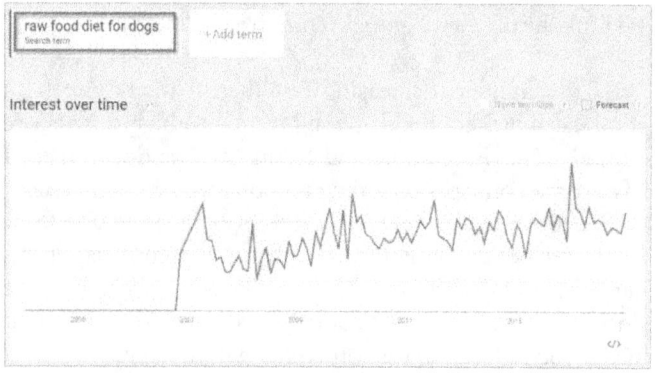

Fig. 22

You can see that this keyword has an upward trend and it has been going up since around 2007 (i.e. from when Google Trends began capturing data for it). So this keyword has better long term prospects than say "raw foods recipes".

12 COMPETITOR ANALYSIS USING FREE TOOLS

Once you've found a possible candidate keyword that passed all previous criteria you now want to analyse the keyword further. The two free tools we use here were introduced in chapter 6.

SEMrush

Link: http://www.semrush.com

We use SEMrush to get a list of websites competing for our keyword and other stats.

In your web browser navigate to http://www.semrush.com and type in "raw food diet for dogs". Then click on SEARCH.

Fig. 23

We get to see a breakdown of data in a series of reports for the following:
- Cost Per Click
- Search Volume
- Trend
- Related keywords and their search volumes
- The top 20 websites ranking for those keywords in search engines like Google

We've already seen some of this data in the Google Keyword Planner but what we're really interested in here is the last one on the list - data on competitor websites in that niche. SEMrush allows us to click on each of the competitor websites and examine specific information about the site.

Our aim is to get into the top 10 on the search engines (specifically on the first page of google) so we're only interested in examining details of the top 10 ranking websites for that keyword.

Fig.24

From the data above I can see that it'll be hard to outrank the first 4 websites due to their prestige and popularity so I would start with the 6th website on the list - rawlearning.com.

Basically with each niche I want to make sure I can be ranking in the top 10 in matter of months.

When you click on one of these links you get some stats that give you an indication whether you would be able to build a site to outrank it within a short time.

You get to see:

Organic search: How much traffic the website gets monthly. The higher this figure the more difficult it is to compete with.

Paid search: If the website is getting traffic from advertising.

Backlinks: How many others sites have links to this website. The higher this figure the more difficult it is to compete with.

Top keywords: The Search Engine (SE) keywords being used to find the site from google. You can get ideas from here for your own site.

Main competitors: The main competitors for this site using the same or similar SE Keywords.

With this information what you're trying to find out is:

Would I be able to build a website to outrank this website in a matter of months?

If the answer is yes then you may not even need to analyse the ones below it. If the answer is no then continue checking the others in the top 10 to see if you can outrank any of them in a matter of months.

MOZ.com

MOZ.com (discussed in Chapter 6) is a free web tool you can use to check figures that determine the "ranking strength" of a website.

Link: https://moz.com/researchtools/ose/

If you enter one of the sites rawlearning.com in MOZ we get the following stats:

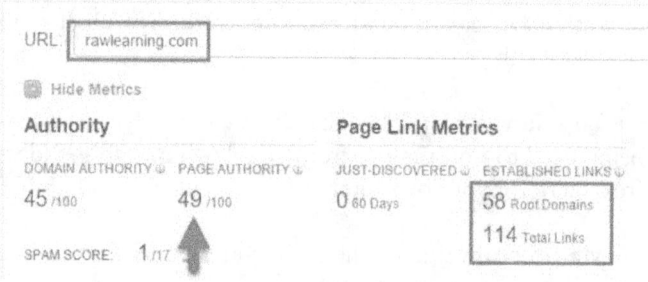

Fig. 25

Domain Authority (DA)

The Domain Authority for a site is scored between 0 and 100. The higher the score the better the site is performing in search engines. You use the Domain Authority to compare sites against each other or in tracking the ranking strength of your website over time. This figure is calculated in Moz by combining a whole raft of figures like number of backlinks, quality of backlinks etc. into a single score.

Page Authority (PA)

The Page Authority has a scale of 0 to 100. The higher the score the better the page is performing in search engines. Page Authority measures the strength of the home page or landing page of the site. For our analysis the Page Authority is the important score to look at.

Established Links

Generally you want to see a "Total Links" figure under 200 for it to be easy to beat. In this case the figure is 96 which is OK.

Analysing the Page Authority

Any site with a PA over 30 will take a lot of hard work to outrank so we are looking for a PA of under 30 for pages in the top 10. In this case the PA is 49 which is quite high and will take too much work to outrank. So we'll have to check the next website on our list of results from SEMrush.com and so on until we find sites with a PA at 30 or under.

Fig. 26

If you see a few sites on the list with their PA less than 30, then you should be able to get into the top 10 in google within a short time, with a bit of work. If you see no sites with a PA of 30 or less then you'll have a hard time competing in the niche and it would be wise to discard that keyword and go back to your Google Keyword Planner results to find another long tail keyword. Then go through this process again.

Think of keyword research as panning for gold. The big gold nuggets have been taken already but there are many smaller ones still there waiting to be found. As Pat

Flynn puts it "The more dirt you get through the better your chance of finding gold."

Now let us see how we can go through this same process using a paid keyword research tool. We'll cover this in the next chapter.

13 COMPETITOR ANALYSIS USING PAID TOOLS

The Google Keyword Planner is free and a great tool for mining for keywords but it only gives us keyword suggestions and search volumes. It doesn't provide analysis on the competition and how easy (or difficult) it is to rank with a particular keyword.

In the previous chapter we used SEMrush and MOZ.com for competitor analysis but as you can see it could be quite cumbersome using so many tools. It can also be very time consuming as it may take several attempts to find a keyword that meets our criteria for a low competition niche.

For many keyword research tasks the Google Keyword Planner will be sufficient but if you want an easier and faster way to carry out competitor analysis on your keywords then you'll have to invest in a paid keyword analysis tool.

There are several of these tools out there in the market but the 2 most popular ones currently in the industry are Market Samurai and Long Tail Pro. I have used both of these tools and my current preference is Long Tail Pro because it is much faster than Market Samurai.

Long Tail Pro

Website: http://www.longtailpro.com

To illustrate how much quicker it is to use Long Tail Pro for the same tasks we carried out in the previous chapter let's type in our seed keyword from the previous chapter "raw food diet" as your main seed keyword.

When you enter the keyword in the software it will generate all the information we got from Google Keyword Planner, including the information from SEMrush.com and MOZ.com for the top 10 search results in Google, all at once!

So you can see straight away that it would save time and the hassle of having to fiddle with different tools and websites.

Also as you get analysis for all the sites at once, you're not reduced to entering them one by one as we had to do with MOZ.com.

Here is an example of the return from the keyword "raw food diet":

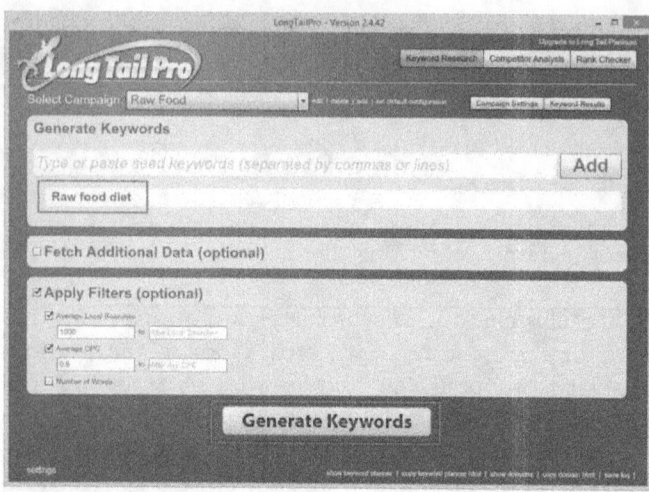

Fig. 27

When you click on Generate Keywords Long Tail Pro connects to Google and other keyword analysis services like MOZ.com and generates results for you, as shown below.

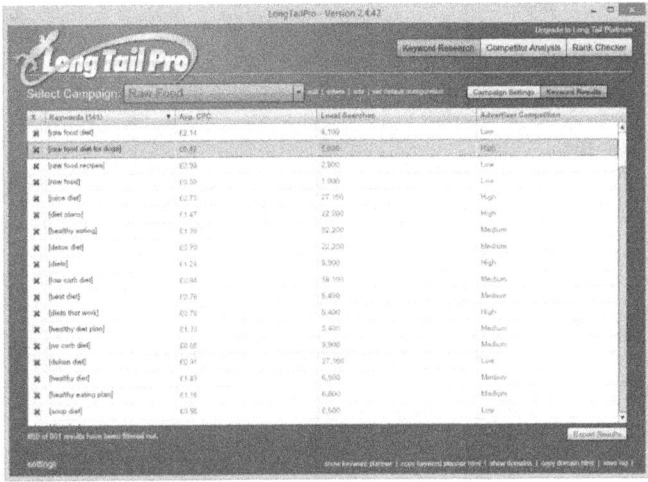

Fig. 28

When you click on the second result "raw food diet for dogs" the software will take you to the Competitor Analysis page and display all the analysis data for that keyword.

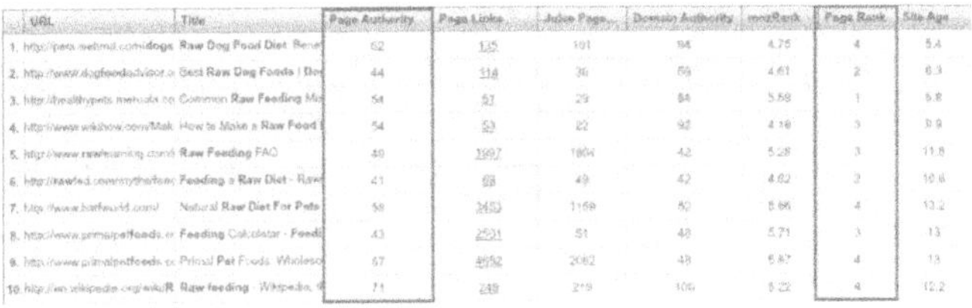

Fig. 29

You can see that the top 10 sites ranking for that keyword and relevant analysis data are displayed in this one window. So with this tool you have a one stop shop for keyword research.

For example you can see the Page Authority (PA) of all 10 sites on one page and you can see straightaway that this keyword will be too competitive to break into the top 10 search results on google. All sites on the list have a PA much greater than 30 (which is the recommended max figure for sites you can realistically outrank within a short period of effort).

Long Tail Pro Columns

Top 10 URLs:

These are the actual pages for the keyword ranking on the first page of Google.

Title:

This is the title of the ranking page in Google. If the keywords appear in the title they're displayed in bold. Having keywords in the title is a strong ranking factor.

Page Authority:

Page Authority predicts the likelihood of a single page to rank well, regardless of its content. The higher the Page Authority, the greater the potential for that individual page to rank well in search results.

Page Rank:

This is a scale from 0 to 10 assigned by Google to signify the overall strength of the page with 10 being the most authoritative. Every page of a website could potentially have a different Page Rank.

MozRank:

According to Moz:

"MozRank represents a link popularity score. It reflects the importance of any given web page on the Internet. Pages earn MozRank by the number and quality of other pages that link to them. The higher the quality of the incoming links, the higher the MozRank.

How is MozRank Scored?

We calculate this score on a logarithmic scale between 1 and 10. Thus, it's much easier to improve from a MozRank of 3 to 4 than it is to improve from 8 to 9. An "average" MozRank of what most people think of a normal page on the Internet is around 3."

Changing Your Seed Keyword

So we've seen that the "raw food diet" niche might just be too competitive for us to build a page we can get to rank in the top 10 of google within a short time. So we can change direction here and search for another seed keyword. For example "gluten free diet".

When we enter this in Long Tail Pro one of the suggestions we get is "yeast free diet" with over 1000 local searches per month.

When we click on this keyword we get the following analysis of the top 10 websites ranking for that keyword.

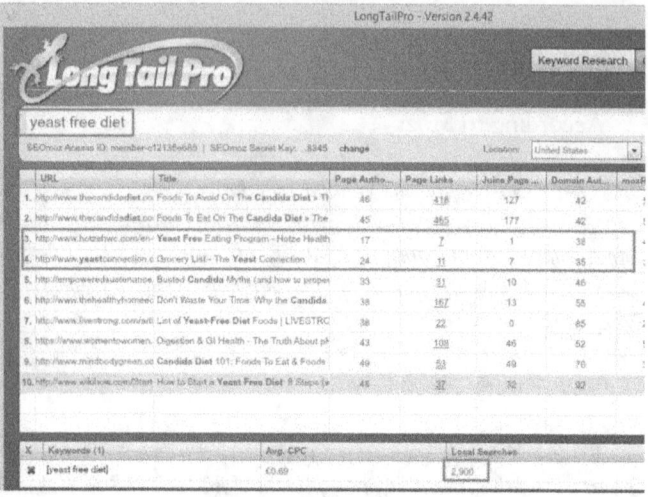

Fig. 30

We can see straightaway that there are two sites in the top 10 list with a Page Authority score of less than 30 that we can compete with and outrank with some effort. If this niche resonates with us we may choose to check the other criteria, mentioned earlier in this book, regarding the profitability of the niche before we proceed to build a website for it.

So with this tool you can see that instead of going through the top ten websites one by one (with the free tools) to get this data, we get it all at once with this software so we can quickly see if we need to go back to the Keyword Research screen and choose another keyword to analyse.

Like panning for gold, we could keep trying different keywords to quickly see if we can rank with them or not. This saves us a lot of time compared to using different tools for the analysis.

If you need to be able to analyse a lot of keywords in the shortest time then a tool like this will save you a lot of time.

14 33 PROFITABLE NICHE IDEAS ANALYSED

The following list is intended to give you brainstorming ideas to help you find a suitable niche online. But please note that it's important to do your own research on top of these ideas. Things change online very quickly so don't simply jump into an area without first researching it.

I have provided some tools in the early part of the book to help you carry out your own research for audience size and analysis of the competition. You still have to do that even with these ideas. In some niches involving finance and health you may need to seek legal advice to establish what you're allowed to do within the rules and regulations.

Niche research is actually fun when you get the hang of it and have the right tools so remember to enjoy yourself.

Health & Fitness

1. Fat Loss

Weight loss is a huge niche but it's too saturated and getting noticed above all the noise can be quite difficult. However fat loss, "cutting" as body builders call it, is a specific area within the weight loss niche. Body builders and physique models who take part in competitions are usually experts at getting "shredded" before competitions i.e. losing fat while retaining muscle. So this is a specialisation. If you have any skills in this department and can differentiate yourself from all the noise in the general weight loss market then you could create products to help people and start a business.

2. Pregnancy

How to deal with pregnancy is not something women learn about in formal education so this is an area where information is highly sought. Women and couples expecting a child or looking to start a family are seeking whatever information they can find.

This is also an area with specialisations where more specific marketing can make your product really stand out and appeal.

For example, we could target particular aspects such as:

- How to get pregnant
- Home birth
- How to eat during pregnancy
- How to lose weight after pregnancy
- Exercise routines
- Breast feeding

- Men's guides to pregnancy
- Financial planning for your new baby

There are lots of eBooks, magazines, blogs, paid ads and affiliate products for this area indicating the niche has potential for making money.

3. Sleep issues

Sleep is a fundamental human requirement and people who have issues in this area will at some point urgently begin to seek solutions. We can see from the popularity of sleeping medications that this is a large problem area and niche you can tap into to provide solutions for people.

The following areas have large search volumes in google:

- Obstructive sleep apnoea
- Sleeping disorder
- Sleep deprivation, Lack of sleep
- Sleep specialist
- How to cure insomnia
- Natural sleep remedies
- How to sleep better
- Snoring solutions

If you have any skills or knowledge in this area, perhaps from finding a solution for yourself at one point, then you can help others by creating an Information Product and sharing your information.

4. Pain

There are different types of pain: Back pain, Joint pain, Arthritis, Migraine etc. and different methods of relieving pain too: Exercise, Stretching, Alexander technique, Yoga, Pilates, Herbal Remedies, Physiotherapy, etc.

This is a big niche and if you are qualified or experienced in helping people deal with one or more of these pain types then you could create an Information Product on the subject like a video course, audio program or an eBook.

5. Yeast Infection

Some conditions that afflict people are hardly catered for in traditional medicine hence many people suffering from conditions like Candida (or other nutritional related problems) often have to seek help elsewhere.

If you have any expertise in this department or found a solution for yourself then your information might be invaluable to many who have the same condition and have been frustrated to no end by traditional medicine.

"Yeast infection" has huge search volumes in the Google Keyword Planner with loads of related keywords with large search volumes too.

6. Specific Skin Conditions

Most skin conditions linked to nutritional imbalances or gut issues are usually auto-immune and this is where most people run into massive frustration with traditional medicine. Traditional medicine usually offers no cures for these conditions and instead provides (usually abrasive) ways to "manage" the symptoms.

Conditions like Seborrheic dermatitis, Eczema,

Psoriasis, Cystic Acne etc. actually still have no official known causes in traditional medicine. So people are forced to seek help and information elsewhere and they often turn to the internet or to nutritionists.

If you have any knowledge about curing or even managing any of these conditions then there are thousands of people out there that you can help. You owe it to yourself to create an Information Product like an eBook on it.

7. Organic foods

Organic foods are becoming more popular due to fears of genetically modified foods along with pesticides and other chemicals. People are seeking more information on organic foods, where to buy organic food, how to grow their own foods, which foods to buy organic, where to eat out organic etc.

If you could set yourself up as an authority in this area then you could build a large following within a short time. There are lots of YouTube channels, blogs, and eBooks dedicated to organic foods and organic living.

8. Cellulite

This is a niche that has been very profitable for many large cosmetic companies. Apart from cosmetics, women are looking for advice like, natural treatment options, prevention techniques and exercise routines to deal with cellulite.

A keyword search using the Google Keyword Planner reveals large search volumes for the following:

- Cellulite treatment

- Cellulite exercises
- Cellulite removal
- Get rid of cellulite
- Best cellulite treatment
- How to get rid of cellulite fast

This is a niche well suited for Information Products like video courses, audio courses or eBooks.

9. Massage

Massage is a popular niche with lots of google searches and paid ads. There are many sub-niches within massage hence lots of areas to create specialist products for.

As an affiliate you could promote massage centres, massage training, massage schools, massage equipment, massage products etc. Massage is also big in sports.

A search with the Google Keyword Planner returns large search volumes for the following:

- Massage products
- Body rub
- Massage for sports
- Spa treatments
- Reiki massage

10. Wellness

Wellness is a "prevention" category as opposed to a "problem" category and people are usually not searching for prevention. Even those searching are not urgently looking for a solution hence it is wise to stay away from prevention categories. However wellness is an exception.

As more people get involved with self-help they're becoming more aware of the limitations of conventional diets and traditional advice regarding feeling well.

More people are now looking for alternatives to conventional methods hence the rapid growth of the health, energy and vitality industry. If you could set yourself up as an authority in this area and capture an audience motivated in wellness it could become a big business for you.

11. Any specific health problem

This is a tricky area as there are often government specific regulations regarding selling or marketing specific "cures" to health problems. Always check the regulations and ensure that you're always within the law.

The fact is that when someone has a specific health challenge, they become very motivated in seeking information about the topic and they're willing to pay for the information. So if you can create an Information Product that helps people solve a specific health issue like, Candida or Seborrheic dermatitis for example, the product can become quite successful.

12. Eating disorders

Eating disorders like anorexia and bulimia are major problems especially in Western society. An eating disorder can quickly become debilitating to the point where the sufferer (or someone close to them) begins to desperately seek solutions.

A keyword search for "Eating disorders" in the Google Keyword Planner comes up with very high search volumes for many phrases related to it. So people are actively searching the internet for information and solutions to deal with this problem.

If you have any information or experience in how to solve eating disorder related problems then there are many people out there you can help and you can reach them via Information Products, a blog or an audio/video course.

Lifestyle

1. Dating Advice

We are wired at birth to grow and seek a mate however many of us face challenges in this area. How to attract a mate may remain a mystery for many people even in adulthood and this may lead them to become highly motivated in seeking solutions.

The dating industry is a multi-million dollar industry and currently quite saturated but there are a lot of sub-niches in this category.

A search with the Google Keyword Planner produces the following phrases with high search volumes:

- Online dating advice
- Dating advice for men
- Dating advice for women
- Christian dating advice
- First date advice
- Relationship advice for women
- Relationship advice for men
- New relationship advice
- Long distance relationship advice

2. Marriage

The ultimate relationship is Marriage. This niche is about improving the quality of married relationships. The offline market for this is huge with many books and counselling services available. On the internet there are thousands of searches performed every month by people looking for help on this subject.

When people get married a lot of things change in their lives as they enter a new phase of their life. With two people things like finances, liabilities, responsibilities, etc. become more complicated.

We're at a time when marriages are failing at an alarming rate, so if you can help people have a successful marriage then you have something valuable to offer.

3. Cooking

The sheer amount of TV shows, magazines, books, celebrity TV chefs etc. shows that cooking is something that a lot of people are passionate about.

The good thing with cooking is that there are so many sub-niches and you can niche down to a specialist area that is not too competitive.

The Google Keyword Planner has a huge volume of searches for the following sub-niches:

- Indian cooking
- Mexican cuisine
- Italian cooking
- Chinese cooking
- Vegan cooking
- Vegetarian cooking
- Gluten free recipes
- Low carb recipes

There are lots of Information Products and physical products on cooking that you could promote as an affiliate like, recipe eBooks, video tutorials, cooking devices and utensils.

4. Divorce

Divorce is the ultimate relationship conflict and unfortunately it is becoming so common that it actually has its own section in some bookstores now. A large group of lawyers focus only on Divorce Law because there is a lot of money to be made in that sector.

As more and more people are going through divorce, market demand for supporting products and services are increasing. This is an area where information is highly sought. If you can help people in this niche then you'll not be short of customers.

5. Retirement

Thanks to the growing number of baby boomers reaching retirement age, this is a growing area, especially in western countries like in North America and Western Europe. More and more people are realising that retirement is coming, that retirement requires money, and that they also have to figure out what to do with all that free time.

If you can help people with information on how to successfully retire or how to deal with the challenges that come up with retirement then you have a good chance of creating a highly profitable business.

The following phrases all have high search volumes in the Google Keyword Planner:

- How to save for retirement
- Retirement planning
- How to retire early
- Best places to retire
- Gated communities

- Senior living

6. Personal Development

The Personal Development industry has been growing for many years as more and more people seek guidance for how to live their lives outside traditional religions.

The success of people like Anthony Robbins, Brian Tracy, Bob Proctor and the popularity of blogs like www.stevepavlina.com, www.lifehacker.com etc. shows how big and lucrative this area is. The market is highly saturated these days of course but the audience is continually growing.

If you plan to enter this market it would be best to have an angle that's not already overplayed in the industry. The possibilities include creating Information Products, one-on-one consultation (maybe over Skype), and mentoring.

As an affiliate you'll not have a shortage of Information Products in online markets like ClickBank and books on Amazon to promote.

7. Golf

Golf is one sport that's doing quite well on the internet in terms of selling stuff. Type in any "golf" related phrase in the Google Keyword Planner and you'll see loads of sponsored ads to do with golf. People are spending a lot of money advertising because there is money to be made. You can do extremely well as an affiliate marketer in this niche if you are interested in golf and can find a sub-niche of it that's not too competitive.

The following have very high search volumes in the Google Keyword Planner:

- Golf shoes
- Golf swing
- Golf clubs
- Golf magazine
- Golf equipment
- Golf accessories
- Golf lessons
- Golf bags

There are a lot of magazines dedicated to golf and this shows that information on the game is highly sought and people are willing to pay for it. If you have any knowledge or interest in golf then you can create Information Products like eBooks and instruction videos.

8. Pets

People tend to be very passionate and emotional about their pets and research has shown that people maintain their spending on pets even through tough economic times. "Dog Training" for example has become a very lucrative niche for Information Products in the last few years.

If you have any expertise in this area an online business is certainly worth exploring. If you are a beginner you may need to find a sub-niche or specialism (like a particular breed of pet) which will enable you to differentiate yourself from the competition and noise in the market.

A search with the Google Keyword Planner reveals large search volumes for the following:

- Puppy training
- Dog obedience training

- German shepherd training
- How to potty train a dog
- Puppy training classes
- Aquarium supplies
- Turtle tanks

Dog training is the most popular right now but there are other niches like fish keeping, horses, cats etc.

9. Photography

If you're into photography then this highly lucrative niche is for you. As an affiliate you can make a lot of money promoting physical products as photography equipment, especially for the pros, can be quite expensive.

You can make a lot of money form AdSense as well as promoting Information Products from ClickBank. Even if you're earning just 4% commission as an Amazon Associate, that could amount to quite a lot of money if products are going for hundreds or even thousands of dollars. One way to promote products as an affiliate is to provide Product Reviews and Comparisons so your free content will be bringing in potential buyers.

10. Music

Music is a top level category with several sub-niches and specialisations. The main areas are Learning Musical Instruments and Music Production. Within these 2 categories there are several sub-niches. A classic example is learning how to play the guitar. Now a niche like that is very broad so you may need to narrow down to a particular kind of guitar for example. People do in this niche when they focus on teaching beginners.

The following phrases related to learning musical instruments come up with high search volumes in google:

- Online piano lessons
- Online guitar lessons
- How to read music
- Violin lessons
- Voice lessons

As for music production there are so many options, from creating your own material, to promoting affiliate products like music making software and hardware.

A search for music production with the Google Keyword Planner returns very high search volumes for the following:

- Music production software
- Recording equipment
- Home recording studio
- Recording studio equipment
- Music production schools

11. Gardening

This is a great niche and a pastime that a lot of people are passionate about. Many people have gardens with all types of plants and flowers they attend to which they regularly seek advice for.

Also, with the growing trend towards organic foods in the Western world, more people are looking for ways to grow their own foods, which is the ultimate in having organic produce.

Popular search phrases in this niche include:

- How to grow tomatoes
- Growing organic vegetables
- Container gardening
- How to grow strawberries
- How to grow potatoes
- Growing garlic
- Hydroponics (growing plants without soil)
- Starting a gardening business
- How to landscape your garden

If you have gardening experience or knowledge in growing your own food then there are a lot of people searching (and willing to pay) for the information you have.

Business And Money

1. Real Estate Investment

Real estate always tends to be a good category for Information Products even though there are boom and bust cycles. In fact you could have more people seeking help and advice when the markets are bad. So an Information Marketer in this niche business will always be steady even in times of recession.

People feel very passionate about real estate and often see it as much more of a solid asset compared to money for example. Perhaps this is what the term "Real Estate" refers to. The audience is very large and there is opportunity for many sub-niches within this niche. You can create a website dedicated to a particular sub-niche of real estate or create an Information Product like a book or video tutorial.

The various areas under this niche include:

- Buy to let
- Houses in Multiple Occupation (HMOs)
- Buying off plan
- Develop/Build
- Refurbishment projects
- International Investments
- How to buy foreclosed properties at auctions
- Real estate "flipping" (buy, fix and sell)
- Tax issues

There are so many niche opportunities within this category and if you have a passion and experience in Real Estate then this can be a very profitable niche to build an online business around.

2. Foreign Currency

One of the most popular forms of trading online is foreign exchange or FOREX trading. This is a very popular niche and fast growing as anyone with some money and an internet connection can start trading online these days. This is no longer the preserve of stock market traders sitting in posh offices in the city.

More people are seeking information and training in this area. So if you have experience and knowledge on how to profit in this market you should consider teaching others by sharing what you've learned in the form of Information Products and earn money in the process.

3. Investing

Stock trading, derivatives, bond investing, penny stock investment, and commodity investment are all very profitable online niches. As more people are doing their own stock trading online the demand for education in this area is also growing.

Have you got any experience in the stock market? If you do then you could teach others what you know by creating and selling Information Products in this niche in the form of eBooks or video courses. Also, if you are interested in this subject but do not have direct experience then you could team up with an expert to create Information Products.

As an Internet Marketer you don't necessarily have to create your products yourself. You could enlist someone who is much better at a particular subject than you to create the content, while you focus primarily on the marketing side. This is the business model of Dummies.com.

4. Internet Marketing

Internet marketing is a highly sought skill because it is an important aspect of doing business online. Everyone doing business online will need to learn Internet marketing skills to be truly successful. Even an author needs to learn online marketing these days to market their books. You could create the best product on a topic but if you don't apply marketing skills in choosing your niche, labelling your product, and promoting your product, then even the best piece of work will register little or no sales.

Unfortunately the market is also full of shady characters promoting "get rich quick" schemes that are worthless and this can sometimes give Internet Marketing a bad name. However there are many genuine marketers in the industry providing high quality and invaluable information like Eben Pagan, Jeff Walker, Frank Kern etc.

If you have gained experience successfully selling stuff online or have mastered a successful formula in a particular area like eBay, YouTube, blogging, Kindle, Amazon, E-Commerce, Information Products etc. then there are many people out there willing to pay for your knowledge.

5. E-Commerce

If you are interested in selling physical products online in places like eBay and Amazon then there are all kinds of services now to make this kind of business a lot easier than it was previously.

There is "drop shipping" for example, where you don't

keep any stocks, but instead forward customer orders directly to the manufacturer and they ship products directly to your customers. You effectively play the role of the middleman without having to handle the physical products yourself. Search for "drop shipping" in Google to learn more about it.

Amazon also now provides a service called Fulfilment by Amazon (FBA) where you store all your stocks at one of their warehouses and they ship all customer orders on your behalf, hence removing the hassle of having to pack and ship orders yourself.

If you are interested in this area then there are many blogs and Information Products out there to teach you how to buy and sell physical products online.

6. Time Management

Time Management is one of the biggest challenges that business people and entrepreneurs face in modern times. As the world gets faster the distractions also multiply. In fact the biggest enemy of business success in modern times is distraction and interruption.

People do not often recognise that better time management is what they need to improve their productivity and this is usually unearthed with deeper probing. This area is one of the big hidden opportunities to create Information Products and coaching to help business people and entrepreneurs.

7. Getting a Job

With the rapidly changing nature of the jobs market, the days of a lifetime career in one company are over. The latest estimates are that by the age of 38 the average University graduate would have gone through 12 different jobs and several career changes.

Knowing how to find a job and succeeding at interviews is increasingly in demand as people are changing jobs more frequently.

If you have any expertise in writing resumes, preparing for interview or how to find work through networking then there are opportunities for you to create Information Products training people in this area.

You could get Camtasia (screen recording software) for example and create a PowerPoint video series on how to succeed at interviews. Then host it at a marketplace like Udemy (marketplace for online courses) and reach millions of people without evening having to create a website.

8. Debt Management

As personal debt increases in society, with the increase in credit cards and loans, the problems that come from having too much debt often lead people to seeking solutions from a place of urgency.

A search with the Google Keyword Tool reveals large search volumes for the following terms:

- How to fix my credit
- Credit repair companies
- Consolidate debt
- Debt consolidation programs
- Debt management program

Debt is one of the growing challenges we face as a society. If you have knowledge that can help people get out of debt and improve their financial health then you certainly should consider creating an Information Product in this area.

9. Starting a Business

Starting a business has never been more accessible to people. With the advent of the internet anyone can now start a business from home. There are millions of people making a full time income running businesses from their homes like - eBay, selling Information Products on ClickBank, Blogs, E-Commerce etc.

As the opportunity to start a business becomes more accessible to more people it is natural that more people are looking for help and advice. People starting their own businesses need some help and hand-holding, whether it's an internet business or a traditional business because business needs hands-on learning.

You can't just read theory and become good at business hence the reason there are no University courses that can teach people how to become entrepreneurs. It needs to be both theoretical and hands-on experience actually doing business in the real world, and this is where people need help and support.

If you are knowledgeable and experienced in this area then you can help others with courses, coaching and mentoring.

10. Money Saving Advice

Looking at the success of sites like MoneySavingExpert.com (a UK based website on money saving tips) it is clear that a lot of people are passionate about saving money and finding the best deals. There are many money saving books and websites because this niche has a large audience.

A search on the Google Keyword Planner reveals a large volume of searches for the following keywords:

- How to save money on groceries
- Frugal living tips
- Money saving tips
- Budgeting tips
- Energy conservation

If you are the kind of person always on the lookout for discounts and bargains, and you know a bit more than the average person on how to get them, then this niche may be ideal for you.

15 FINAL THOUGHTS

To summarise, you don't get to decide on what niche to enter or what business to start. Rather, the market decides for you. You look at the market to see what's selling, what people are currently spending money on. Within that criterion you then find what resonates with you.

In a way this makes it easier to find projects to work on as we don't have to agonise and deliberate for ages on what to do, as can often be the case. The market decides for us.

When you find a profitable niche that resonates with you the next step is to check if you can actually be competitive in the niche and get noticed. A niche that's too saturated, where it's difficult to stand out from the crowd, is just as bad as a niche with no customers.

Finding the right niche is the most crucial part of online business success because if you get this wrong then nothing else works. On the other hand if you get this right then everything else just falls in place naturally.

As I mentioned before, instead of trying to create a cash stream, find a cash stream that's already flowing and position yourself in the right place for some of it to flow towards you.

Wishing you all the best for your entrepreneurial future!

ABOUT THE AUTHOR

Nathan George graduated from Birkbeck, University of London with a degree in Information Systems and Management. He worked for 14 years as an analyst/programmer and website developer in the IT services industry in the UK before venturing out into the dotcom world as a digital entrepreneur. He currently runs several niche websites making revenue through affiliate marketing and advertising. He is also interested in independent publishing and the various tools and systems available to indie authors.